CLEVEDON PIER

A celebration of England's finest pier

Clive Minnitt

To my dear sister Jane and her daughter Laura,
who tragically lost their lives so young.

This book is for you both.

Beautiful iron pier of the silvery sea
All your numerous arches and pillars are so grand to me
And pagoda and legs which seem to the eye
To be almost reaching up to the sky.
The greatest wonder it must be
And a great beautification to the Severn Sea
Most beautiful may I boast
Near by Clevedon and the Somerset coast.

Mike Lord

After the poem, *An Address to the New Tay Bridge*,
by William Topaz McGonagall
(apologies to McGonagall – MFL).

CONTENTS

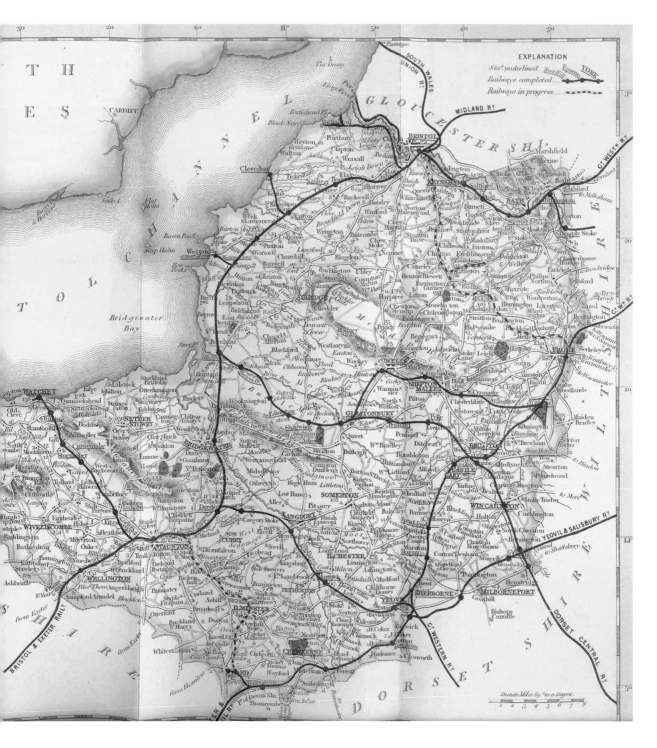

This map was published in a book called the *New Handbook of Clevedon*, written in 1864, and donated to Clevedon Library by Mary Seeley of 'Foxwood', Towerhouse Lane, Wraxall. The presence of the excellent railway links spurred on the building of the pier in order to provide onward travel to South Wales by steamer.

Contents   5

GRIFF RHYS JONES

I am drawn to piers. Aren't we all? The airy suspension of that bridge to the sea, with the open gaps, the painted railings, the impossible elevations and the glimpses of the British water far below: yellowy brown and slightly confused. They are walkways leading nowhere. Or, at least, that's what I thought when I was little. My father always sailed his little boat right past the ends of Clacton or Walton Pier and we had to go back from the landward end. And I was only interested in the waltzer then. It wasn't until I was older that I understood the significance of the long reach out to sea.

When I was eight I took the paddle steamer from Cardiff with my Aunty Gwen. We went all the way to Ilfracombe and then on to Lundy Island. It was a beautiful day. I wonder, did we pull up at Clevedon Pier and make use of it as it should be used: as a landing stage? I rather think we might have, because when I came back years later to film it for television, it certainly felt like somewhere I had been before. It was the pier of fantasy. It was the pier of dreams. Costing £10,000 to build in 1868 and, so they tell me, made of second hand rails, Clevedon Pier soars above the water like a cat's cradle. The pagoda at the end of the 869ft is so aptly judged, so perfectly poised, it looks made of icing sugar. It is odd to think that it was added later. The whole confection may have been an accident, but what a happy one. I can think of few Victorian structures that have such a timeless architectural and engineering perfection and yet at the same time such frivolity. And yet there aren't any slot machines or bumper cars on this pier. I would have been disappointed as a six year old, but even a six year old could see that Clevedon Pier is somehow an epitome of light-hearted seaside fun itself. Thank goodness it was saved. Thank goodness for English Heritage and the National Heritage Lottery Fund. Thank goodness for all those hardworking fundraisers and supporters who put such efforts into preserving it. And what a marvellous subject for photography.

Here is a wonderful record of all its moods. Being light and airy itself, it invites the light and air to enfold it. As the seascape changes, so does the mood of the pier. Clive Minnitt's photographs capture that. Long may Clevedon Pier stretch out to infinity and beyond.

We came to Clevedon before World War II, in 1937. My father skippered boats and we always loved being by the sea. Even before we moved from Cardiff on the Campbell's boat, we used to visit the town and I remember having confetti battles on the end of the pier. My mother would make me undress in the cart shed so that I wouldn't leave a trail of colourful paper throughout the house. Jenny Pritchard

INTRODUCTION

Early days

It was the arrival of the railway in the 19th century that highlighted the need for a pier in Clevedon, which would in turn give access to steamers and onward travel to and from south Wales. On Easter Monday, 29 March, 1869, the completion of the pier's construction was celebrated. It enjoyed much success over the next century, but its importance was gradually diminished by a series of events. The building of a rail tunnel under the River Severn and the construction of the Severn Suspension Bridge to accommodate the vast increase in road traffic helped to bring about eventual failure.

Disaster struck in 1970, when part of the pier collapsed – ironically, while undergoing load-bearing tests, which were necessary to gain insurance certification. Only through clever legal representation, much lobbying by local pressure groups, and intense fundraising was it possible to save the pier from demolition. Even then, the financing of the planned restoration might well have proved insurmountable had it not been for substantial help from English Heritage and a grant from the Heritage Lottery Fund, in addition to generous donations from many other bodies.

The final piece in the jigsaw saw the fully restored pier officially opened on May 23rd, 1998 – a great tribute to all those who had fought for its survival. The ultimate accolade of becoming only one of two piers in the country to be awarded the Grade I listed status was received in 2002. The other, the West Pier in Brighton, has sadly had its own share of bad luck in recent years, having suffered both a major collapse and two suspected arson attacks.

January 2nd, 1997, was a monumental day in my life. Two weeks earlier I had been employed in the IT department of a major player in life assurance. Leaving celebrations, hangovers and the Christmas and New Year festive season had passed. Day one in the life of the latest person to join the ranks of the world's freelance photographers had arrived.

Lady Luck often has her say in the most unexpected ways. A 'nothing ventured nothing gained' phone call to introduce myself somewhat tentatively to a small but successful public relations company in the heart of Bristol's rapidly expanding commercial quarter, resulted in a working relationship that was ultimately to lead to many exciting projects.

"A woman complained that there was no lift facility at the pier head to take people up and down to the steamers at low tide. She obviously didn't realise that the lift would be submerged for much of the time." 'Taxi' Tim Vine

My brief was that I should provide images for the front cover and inside pages related to one of the featured articles of the re-vamped Link, a business magazine for the west of England. The 1997 winter edition was to feature the ongoing restoration of a local well-known landmark under the banner, 'Clevedon Pier – Victorian gem resurrected'. I quickly learned that owning a camera was akin to having a passport – it enabled me to visit places I would not have been allowed into otherwise. A courteous phone call helped me obtain the necessary permission for access to what was, in essence, a building site.

Although the majority of the pier had been restored, there was still much work to do on the reconstruction of the Victorian pier head pagoda and outer buildings. The pier itself resembled an obstacle course. Scaffolding, steel rods, general mess, workmen up to their armpits in rivets, schedules and budgets. It was a forlorn-looking novice professional photographer who struggled to find that elusive dramatic image which would grace the magazine's front cover and, in turn, please the editor. The protective hat I was asked to wear ensured that the gap between the camera's viewfinder and my left eye was far greater than was practical. I remember thinking: "Photographers don't wear silly hats" – a thought I have retracted many times since!

My front cover image stayed with me for many years and has always intrigued me. It suddenly dawned on me during a subsequent visit to the pier, early in February 2007 (when I decided to use the pier as the subject for an article for Outdoor Photography magazine) that here was a superb location on which to concentrate my photographic efforts. Better still, it was on my doorstep.

Coincidentally, Linda Strong, the pier manager, had purchased a photograph of the Second Severn Crossing many years ago and we had not met since. Fortunately, she was very enthusiastic about my idea of producing a book about the pier and successfully sought permission from the trustees for me to go ahead.

Why a book?

The majestic setting of Clevedon Pier affords outstanding views of the coastlines of north Somerset and across the Severn Estuary to south Wales. The islands of Steep Holm and Flat Holm can be seen to the southwest and the two impressive road crossings, the Severn Suspension Bridge and the Second Severn Crossing are also within viewing distance upstream.

I cannot help but be impressed with the way the area close to the pier has had its Victorian character largely retained. I am not alone. The late Sir John

Betjeman, poet laureate from 1972 until his death in 1984, had a great love for architecture and commented that the pier was: "The most beautiful pier in England and without its pier, Clevedon would be a diamond with a flaw."

His words were influential in helping to save the pier from demolition. The landscape artist, JMW Turner, would paint the remarkable sunsets. Coleridge, Lord Tennyson, and many others who excelled with the written word, were also inspired whenever they visited Clevedon.

The pier has been the subject of several excellent published books in the past (see Further Reading), which have been largely related to historical or construction matters. The last of these was completed in 1995. After such a long gap I felt the time was right for me to try and use my skills to produce a collection of images which show the pier in a different light, if you will excuse the pun.

After only a few visits it was obvious that not only was the pier a rather special subject in its own right, but that the small bay which lay next to it was also a wonderful source of subject matter. Geological wonders abound, and seaweed, surf, a pebbled beach and the second highest tidal range in the world were just a few of the natural elements which, if used in a considered way in conjunction with the nearby pier, would provide me with a wealth of photographic possibilities.

It didn't stop there. There were hardy swimmers, sailing boats, crabbers, romantic couples, fun and frolics. On the pier, the fishermen who braved all weather imaginable. Not to mention the 9,000 or so brass plaques which have

been attached to the planks and backs of seats to commemorate, celebrate or simply acknowledge others, past and present.

As the photography progressed, I became aware that there were many people with a story to tell. They would start to relate their experiences about life on or near the pier, on the water or dry land. I thought how appropriate it would be to combine some of their tales with my photography, and ideas for the book content began to form.

The benefits of producing this book are intended to be many. From a photographic angle, I wanted to show the potential that such a small area has in providing outstanding subject matter. This proved to be a very enjoyable and rewarding challenge.

The Clevedon Pier and Heritage Trust is a registered charity, and has to rely solely on generating its own income and constant fundraising efforts to keep the pier and tollhouse in existence. With luck, sales of this book will help the fundraising process and help pay for a few more nuts and bolts to be painted during the next round of maintenance activity.

A third important reason for documenting the current beauty of the pier and beach is that future generations will be able to see what this section of the Bristol Channel looked like in the early part of the 21st century. In years to come it is quite possible that a barrage will be built across the Severn Estuary to provide electricity. If it does go ahead then the tidal flows will be altered and an entirely different eco-scene may develop.

It is my dearest wish that you enjoy reading this book and might be sufficiently moved to take your own camera for a walk and see what is just around the corner.

A few photographic considerations

Part of my work takes me to various parts of the world, leading photographic holidays with my good chum and fellow photographer, Phil Malpas. People assume that because I travel regularly it goes without saying that I will always find something to photograph or that the light is so much better in Outer-Los-Venizia-by-the-sea-de-Janeiro. Although there is some truth in this, I'm convinced that Britain is one of the best places on the planet for the quality of light. The landscape photographer could not be more fortunate. Although our climate is changing, we still have four distinct seasons as opposed to the 'wet' and 'dry' versions experienced by many others, and 'our' sun rises and sets much more slowly than when observed nearer the equator.

In the UK, the photographer benefits from changing times of dawn and dusk through the year, incredible tidal ranges, 11,000 miles of coastline, and extremely varied scenery and architecture. Our weather patterns are varied to say the least.

However, these and many other reasons not mentioned here, do not mean that generating enough high quality images to produce a book is easy. Far from it. But if the raw materials are present then the enjoyable part can begin. It might require several visits before the subject is seen at its optimum. Some of the images in this book were taken on the hoof, reacting to what was seen. Many of them were previsualised and the times of my visits planned to coincide with the conditions I had seen in my mind. Some images needed many visits to achieve – and a few have still not been, and may never be, realised.

One of the most important things I have learnt about photography is that it's not the subject we are photographing but the interplay it has with light. It may be light falling on it or reflecting off it. It could be that a dull, overcast day is best. Even the most mundane subjects will stand out when shown in the right light. Clevedon Pier makes an exceptional subject and offers much for the photographer.

It was never my intention to produce a 'blue sky' tourist book, but to attempt to show the pier, beach and Bristol Channel in some of the many moods I have experienced. The challenge has been to match the right light with the right subject at the most suitable time of day. I hope I have succeeded.

I have met many helpful people while photographing for this book, almost all of whom have had a tale or two to tell. I am indebted to them all. When asked what the pier means to them, the response has usually been: "Well, just look for yourself…"

This project has been a wonderful journey, not all plain sailing by any means. There have been moments when I have questioned my own sanity. But finally, its conclusion means that I am able to contribute towards celebrating the finest English pier. For that I am grateful.

"The vicar was in a wheelchair and wanted to scatter a person's ashes over the side of the main deck. Normally it would be done from the pier head, but he insisted it be done from the deck. I told him if that was the case, then he must do it from the starboard side. He didn't – and the ashes blew back into his hair. His moustache was covered. His son had to ask for a brush and vacuum cleaner to help clean him up."
Maggie Ashford

"Heavy seas and storm force winds have the potential to wreak havoc on the sea front, although the area has escaped relatively lightly over the years. In the 1980s there was flood damage to some of the properties to the rear of the beach - a few half-submerged vehicles and the sea wall had to be rebuilt. The pier has occasionally suffered, usually when we get spring tides and high winds together. The waves are whipped up under the pier and sometimes rip planks off their moorings, particularly at the end of the pier nearest the tollhouse.

On one occasion a number of planks were torn off and swept along with the tide to Ladye Bay, about a mile upstream. They were salvaged by a kind soul who returned the plaques which had been attached to the planks - but not the planks! Thankfully, the pier master at the time had kept a record of the plaque details, and those that hadn't been washed ashore could be remade.

The first section of the pier had to be altered to so that the planks were sitting on a framework. This meant they could be removed whenever the weather and sea looked threatening." 'Taxi' Tim Vine

A WIDER VIEW

It has been said on more than one occasion that Clevedon Pier is the most elegant in the country. Many Victorian piers were constructed around the coast of England but, of those that still exist, arguably none has quite the same sleek, proud appearance as Clevedon's architectural gem.

The pier acts as a beacon as it projects almost 900ft into the Bristol Channel. A most satisfying way to enjoy a first view of the pier is to arrive by foot along the coastal routes, either from Portishead in the north or the southerly Poets' Walk. From a personal stance, that first sighting always generates a feeling of excitement and I usually have to force myself to walk at a slower pace so that I can savour the moment.

I must have studied the pier from every conceivable angle, apart from the rear seat of a microlight plane. A few years ago I wouldn't have hesitated if the opportunity had arisen for me to take to the air in one. Now I would be much more at home enjoying the relative safety of a more sedate hot air balloon ride. Unfortunately, my dream of flying over the pier in a wicker basket powered by a following light, easterly breeze usually turns into a nightmare as the gas runs out half way across the estuary.

My aim was to show the pier in the context of its surroundings and in some of its many moods. From the outset, planning trips from my Bristol home was vital. For instance, I had to be sure that 2007 hadn't been designated a 're-painting the pier' year. Imagine arriving in Australia to fulfill a commission to photograph the Sydney Opera House only to find that it was covered in scaffolding! Not a fair dinkum idea and a very expensive mistake.

On numerous occasions I have studied the tide times and heights for the Bristol Channel, not to mention sunrise and sunset times. The position of the sun at sunrise and sunset varies substantially throughout the year and a general guide to photographing at dawn and dusk is that those subjects which face north are best visited in the summer and south facing subjects saved for the winter months. The pier faces northwest and, as it can be viewed from north, south and east, any time of year is suitable, particularly at dusk.

Weather forecasts are useful but can be misleading. There is a saying in photographic circles: "There is no such thing as poor weather, only a poor subject." Occasionally I postponed my 15-mile journey for a dawn shoot after hearing a wretched forecast – but only after I had got out of bed to have a look

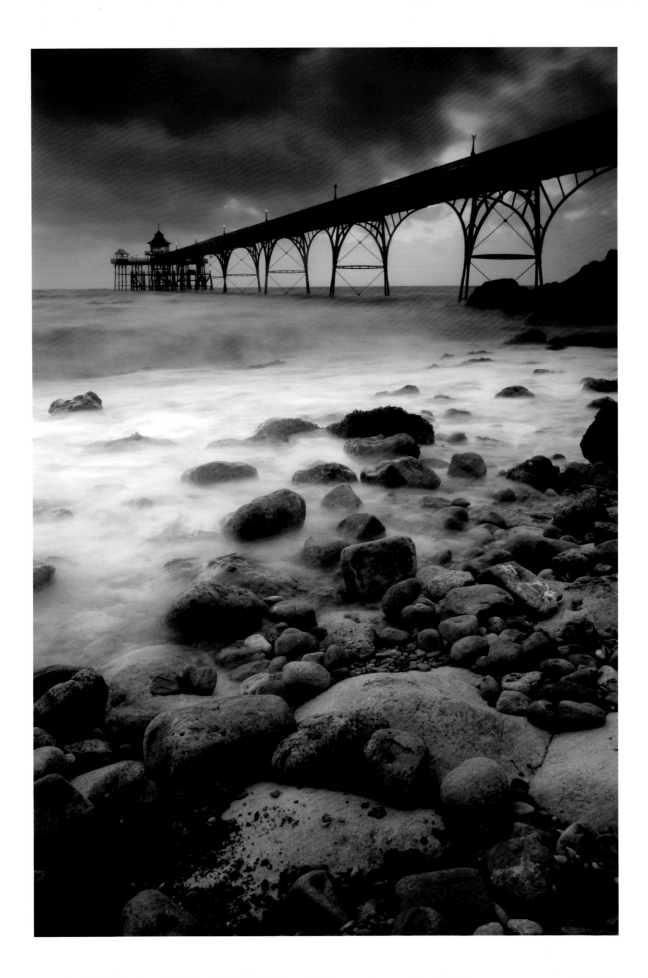

"About 40 years ago, I used to take my daughter to the end of the pier to have a sausage roll. The pier collapsed after one visit. She was so concerned, she asked: 'What about the sausage rolls, what will happen to them?'" Doug Gregory

"It was a hot, sunny day. My family and I had just been for a knickerbocker glory in a nearby café. The pier was huge – scary, but exciting. My sister and I hopped over the gaps between the creaking floorboards thinking we would fall through at any moment. I'm 14 years older now and stepping on to the pier still gives me that tingle of excitement." Alexandra Webber

for myself. Generally it would depend on what I had planned to photograph. A windy day would put paid to any reflections and any photography on the pier using a tripod and long shutter speed would be impossible – but the same conditions might be perfect for a wider view taken from the beach.

Each image was the result of a decision-making process, often carried out subconsciously in seconds. Should I include more sky than sea or land or vice versa? Do I need to include anything else in the foreground? Would it be better to have the tide in or out, or perhaps somewhere in between? What time of day should I photograph it? How about some rough waves – or is a calm sea more suitable? Would it help if there were a passing ship in the scene? Most importantly, what am I seeking to do with these images and what am I trying to say?

Frequent visits allowed me the luxury of being able to try all of these different approaches. My eagerness sometimes got the better of me and I ended up being semi-drenched when edging too close to crashing waves. The thick mud, for which the seabed in this part of the Severn Estuary is renowned, certainly challenged me when attempting to reach some of the more difficult viewpoints. It did me good to step out of my comfort zone and endure some arduous conditions and each successful image made the adventure worthwhile.

I have never felt comfortable working in strong wind and rain. During my childhood I lived on an old army camp where my parents had a chicken farm – a great place for my sister and me to grow up. The house was part of what was previously the hospital block, and made of wood – my rabbits lived in the

"Sarah Jane was sitting on the pier with a man who, I think, was a nephew. She was sitting on the starboard side, about half way down, gazing across to the Welsh coast. She seemed to be deep in thought, but I felt bound to stop and talk to her. She told me about the old days - and I mean old, because she told me she was 101 years old. She looked beautiful in a smart, edge-to-edge royal blue coat, a crisp white blouse with real pearl buttons, and a bow at the nape of her neck. She had a straw hat perched at a slightly jaunty angle on top of her pure white hair. Her hat was blue to match her coat. Her shoes were neat and clean and sported a little heel; in fact, she looked perfectly turned out and certainly not as old as her years. She told me that she lived in Wales and her husband used to come over to Clevedon to imbibe, when drink was forbidden on Sundays in their country. When he was due home she would go down to meet the paddle steamer's return, because she knew he would be the worse for wear. She would take the yard broom with her to help push her husband up the hill to their home and, when the two of them reached the back gate, she would lock him in the garden shed until he sobered up. 'You see', she said in a lovely Welsh lilt, 'we had three daughters and I would never have let them see their father in a drunken state.' What absolute pride, I thought. She let me take her photo and posed for me. A significant feature of this lovely lady was her feet. They didn't reach anywhere near the deck, and she had to wriggle to get off the seat. But what a powerful lady she was. When she left the pier, she said to me: 'Goodbye now, and remember, I'm Sarah Jane and I am very special.'" Maggie Ashford

morgue. When there were gales my bedroom walls would move in and out, creaking loudly. I was convinced the house would collapse on top of me. It never did!

Among my most exciting visits to the pier were those that coincided with the arrival of the Balmoral pleasure steamer. Built in 1949, it is a fantastic sight. However, my extra special ingredients were light, water, rock and clouds. Apart from the rocks, they all changed constantly. But the rocks were affected by changes in the other elements. By anticipating the next move of each natural element rather than reacting to them, I was able to use them in conjunction with the pier.

As ever, there were times when it didn't all come together. When it didn't, I learnt the answer to the burning question, what do fishermen and photographers have in common? The answer: they all harp on about the one that got away. Mine was the Waverley – the last seagoing paddle steamer in the world. Each time she visited I was elsewhere, with camera of course!

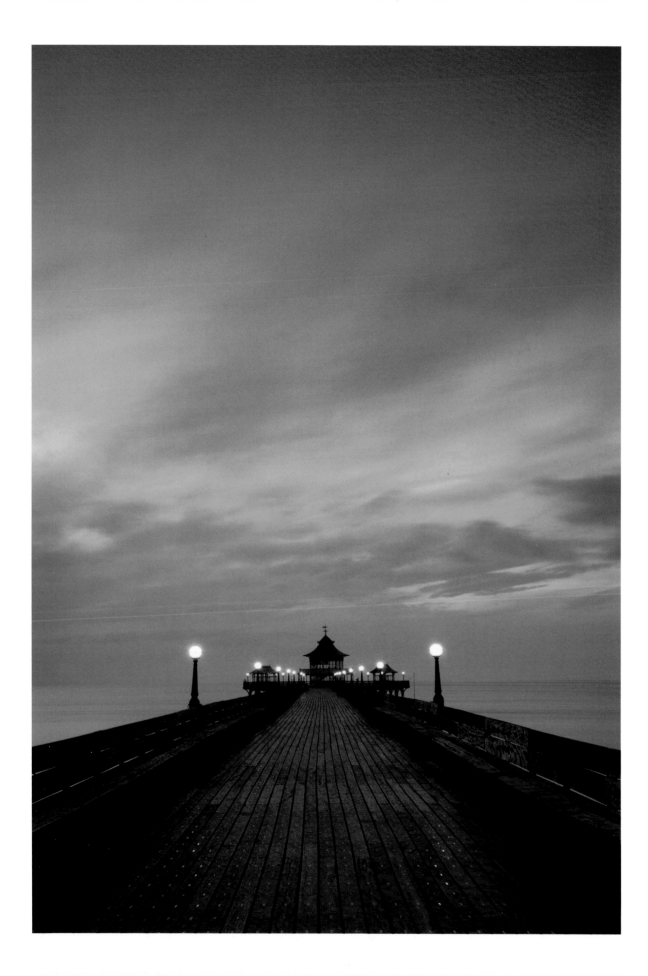

"On three occasions during my time at the pier, the Waverley went
to the rescue of a small vessel in the channel, picking up survivors
and towing the boat back to Clevedon. I remember that the same
man was picked up on two occasions, but with a different woman
each time. He was not amused because we took pictures of them
and sent them to the press. In fact, he didn't even say thank you for
being rescued, and I doubted whether he would attempt any more
romantic dalliances at sea without first taking a few lessons in
navigation." Maggie Ashford

"When the reconstruction work was being carried out at the far end of the pier, visitors were taken over by boat to have a look at the progress. The females among them got a bit of a surprise when they climbed up onto the pier head to find the workers wearing their tool belts and nothing else." Mary Buck

MOODS OF THE BRISTOL CHANNEL

The Bristol Channel has a claim to fame. A sign on the side of the tollhouse building states: 'The tide range at this pier is the second highest in the world. On spring tides there is a rise of over 47ft from low water.'

Few people know where the highest range is located, but the general consensus points to the Bay of Fundy, which lies between the Canadian provinces of New Brunswick and Nova Scotia and has a tidal range of more than 16m, or 52ft.

The funnelling of the sea up the Severn Estuary into the narrowing Bristol Channel gives rise to another natural phenomenon, known as the Severn Bore – not a sad and lonely photographer, but a tidal wave which can reach a height of up to two metres. If you stand on the pier during particularly high spring tides, you can feel the moment it rattles through. It is more evident along the higher reaches of the river towards Gloucester, where the river twists and turns and narrows considerably. The narrowing of the river similarly exaggerates the effect and produces sufficiently high waves, and the ensuing surge of water has become a challenge for windsurfers and canoeists for several miles upstream. Thousands flock to watch the spectacle, risking a good soaking into the bargain.

The moods of the channel are many. The famous Clevedon sunset, which has inspired artists, writers and poets, usually marks my starting point for an enjoyable session of photography at dusk. A sinking ball of fire is like a magnet to millions around the world as they rush to capture one final image before packing the camera away the moment it dips below the horizon. However, the following 30 to 40 minutes invariably promise much more in the way of atmospheric conditions. This precious time is known as 'afterglow' and has left me speechless on many occasions – something my friends might be surprised to read.

There have been moments when I wished I could stop time. November 15th, 2007 saw dusk coincide with low tide and the tops of several sandbanks were revealed. The light was incredible, the wet sandbanks glistened in the channel and both the sea and sky featured myriad orange, red, purple, mauve and blue hues. The north Somerset coast and the island of Steep Holm were silhouetted in the distance. A written description cannot possibly do it justice. If I hadn't been concentrating so hard, I might have overheard the odd marriage proposal.

Talking of coming over all misty – a thick fog lying over the channel might be atmospheric, but it is difficult to photograph well. If the pier head buildings can be seen poking up through the mist the possibilities are far greater. If it is light fog or, even better, a few whispers of mist with a low angled single ray of light, plus the pier lights illuminated, and then an albatross – well…

There is nothing better than to watch and feel a violent sea. An appreciation of its immense power can be felt while standing on the pier head during a storm. It is exhilarating, awesome and frightening. You feel the full force of nature as the sea surges past the elegant legs of the pier on its way upstream. Although the pier has survived many storms, early spring tides coupled with high winds can wreak havoc with the sea front. It can become a dangerous place. After such storms, out come the cameras and the shutter clicking can be heard for miles. I, too, love a good storm, especially when there are dramatic skies and thunderous clouds above. The sound of the sea crashing on the shore is a cathartic experience. The artistic side kicks in and, using a range of apertures, focal lengths and shutter speeds, gives me the chance to generate some interesting images using the movement of the water as the focal point of the scene.

In contrast, the calm, reflective mood generated at high tide when there is little or no wind, is therapeutic. An overcast sky, not the dull grey type most of us loathe, but a mixture of pastel blues, greys and pinks, lulls one into a feeling of wellbeing and contentment. I can imagine myself falling asleep and getting no photography done whatsoever.

Despite many visits to the Clevedon sea front, the weather has not always played along with my advance written requests. I still have to witness a rainbow over the pier against a dark and foreboding sky, seen from the shore. On one occasion, I experienced the phenomenon from the pier head looking back towards land, but it didn't have the desired effect. Neither have I seen a lightning storm over the channel. I have seen several exceptional images of lightning strikes by some of the world's experts, which makes me realise how difficult it is to perfect. As with all landscape photography, there is an element of luck, but it's an art form in itself and requires a high degree of skill. Practice makes perfect. Perhaps I should live in the tropics where electrical storms are much more frequent.

"In the 1960s I used to go fishing on the pier - day and night - so often it almost became my home. I regularly caught cod, whiting, sole and skate. I remember fishing on a very stormy day, during a particularly high tide. The pier was buffeted by ferocious winds and waves, and the seafront road was bombarded with seawater. I felt it would be wise to return to shore after seeing lots of wooden planks torn off the landing stage and dumped in the sea. Conditions were far too dangerous to be out on the pier. When I was two-thirds of the way back to dry land, some of the pier decking was ripped up in front of me. Waves were blowing up through the gaping holes. I retreated along the pier until the tide had subsided and chose my moment to run to safety along the seating which lines the side of the pier." Alf Watts

"January 3rd, 2007 was a dark day, and the weather forecast was bleak: heavy rain and high winds coming up the Bristol Channel from the west. Little did we know, when they said gales they really meant gales. By 1pm, the wind had reached a force that made us consider closing the pier. To my surprise, a fisherman appeared at the tollhouse, keen to go fishing. As the wind was still increasing I decided it was too dangerous to allow anyone onto the pier. He was none too pleased and said the wind was due to subside in the afternoon.

Over the next hour and a half the winds confirmed my decision. Swansea coastguard informed us that a force ten was blowing through the channel and a gust of 53 knots (60mph) had been recorded. Slates were blown off the tollhouse roof and the finials that adorn the flagpoles were being torn from the tops of the poles along the sea front. They're made of brass and would cause serious injury if they hit anyone.

The waves crashed over the top of the promenade and left huge deposits of seaweed, and the gates at the pier entrance began to rattle with such force I feared my car would be demolished if they were torn from their hinges. I had to ban the staff from venturing outside for fear of them being hit by the flying tiles. We watched the waves crash against the sea walls and pound the shingle along the beach. Finally, the winds subsided enough to allow us to go home. The next morning the force of the storm was clearly visible. Strewn along the beach were large branches, plastic drums, seaweed and a big wheel, probably from a tractor. Clevedon in a storm is an exciting place to be." Linda Strong

"My wife Valerie and I have, for many years, visited Clevedon on Sunday afternoons. We usually park in Hill Street and wander along the shops. Hill Street is so nostalgic – the shops are, almost without exception, privately owned, and a refreshing change from the stereotypical high streets of today. We continue to Clevedon Pier – surely Britain's finest, and the only intact Grade I listed pier remaining. After walking along the pier and taking in the views of the Bristol Channel, we cross the road to Scarlett's Café for an ice cream, sitting outside enjoying the ozone from the channel and the ice cream from Cold Ashton.

There is a strong Victorian atmosphere to this bay in Clevedon, which we enjoy. Memories of Val's holidays when she was a child come flooding back as we walk past what was known then as Esplanade House – renowned for excellent food even during rationing. Retuning along Hill Street we are once again refreshed by an afternoon of nostalgia, fresh air and a little exercise." Peter Ruck

"After spending a day out on the Waverley, a woman complained that the windows of the paddle steamer were covered in sea spray."

'Taxi' Tim Vine

ON THE WATER

What is it about the presence of water that brings out the child in so many of us? During most weekends, the sea front is buzzing with activity, particularly at high tide.

It was New Year's Day. I had been in Clevedon for a few hours setting up an exhibition in the pier's tollhouse gallery. Looking through the window, I was puzzled by the sight of what looked like a cannon being positioned on the beach, just above high water. Large crowds were gathering on the esplanade and I could see some strange goings-on taking place. A number of people were dressed as pirates and were making their way towards the shore where there was a plank waiting to be walked. I thought to myself, "Rather you than me," especially as it was the middle of winter and the water temperature was only seven degrees.

I like quaint old English customs (and fancy dress for that matter) but this one left me feeling out of my depth. The impressive cannon, made from a length of piping which had been washed onto the beach, was fired on several occasions. The final blast signalled it was time to discard pirate outfits and don swimming togs, and a sizeable portion of the population of Clevedon applauded the brave souls as they launched themselves into the channel. A real community spirit prevailed.

I'm full of admiration for these hardy folk. Not only do a number of swimmers enjoy a dip most days of the year, but some of them are local legends as a result of their aquatic exploits. Len Hurley has competed in an incredible 50 consecutive years of the Clevedon Long Swim – a one-mile course from Ladye Bay to the beach near the pier. Steve Price set new standards, becoming the first person to swim across the Bristol Channel and back in one go. He has also swum the English Channel and the Irish Sea, admittedly with a break between the two. At 16 years of age, Gary Carpenter has recently become the youngest person to swim the 18 miles from Penarth in south Wales to Clevedon. In each case it was the sight of the pier that inspired them to achieve their goals.

"During one race, a salmon leapt into a boat and the crew member held it aloft, shouting to the nearest boat: 'Look what we've caught!' His skipper told him in no uncertain terms to throw it back in. 'We're racing!' he said." **Sailing club**

Weekends also see the sailing flotilla out on the water. Brightly coloured sails billowing in the wind provide exciting opportunities for the photographic fraternity. As with swimming, sailing time is limited by the tide and the infamously strong currents, to just a short period either side of high tide. As I trailed their movements with my lens, I felt I was almost out there with them, bobbing up and down on the waves.

Photographing moving subjects is an art in itself and it's great fun to experiment with different techniques. Even before taking the camera out of my bag, I would be asking myself what I was trying to convey. Did I want to show a subject moving against a blurred background? If I wanted to create an image where every element was static, where every droplet of water splashing off the dinghy's bow appeared pin sharp, what shutter speed should I use? What do I need to do if it's too dark to use a fast shutter speed?

When photographing the boats, my preferred vantage point is the higher ground. This also gives me a better angle when trying to create an image which includes backlit sails. When this happens, it is breathtaking to watch. It also gives me more scope when being creative with my compositions. Generally speaking, an odd number of elements help to make a much more successful composition than an even number. For instance, one, three or five boats is more pleasing on the eye than two or four. But that isn't the end of it, as simply including them doesn't improve anything unless they are placed in such a way as to be meaningful. Equally as important as these elements is the space left between each of them. There has to be a balance – not necessarily symmetrical, but where the elements are not fighting each other for position.

Besides all the fun and games of swimming and sailing, huge container ships can be seen in the distance as they ply their way to and from Avonmouth and Royal Portbury docks. What a contrast when compared with the elegance of the pier, apparent fragility of the sailing boats, canoeists and occasional windsurfer. When combining a number of these in a photograph, I have tried to work on the 'balance' principle I have just mentioned. That's half the fun.

"I'm 73 now and I've been swimming for 50 years. There are about 20 of us in the club and probably six or seven go in the water every day. On an incoming tide we swim out towards the buoys and the tide brings us back. On an outgoing tide we swim out under the pier and return on the tide."

Doug Gregory

"After three lads had enjoyed a few sherbets at the Moon and Sixpence pub, one of them decided to do a Reginald Perrin, stripping off to his underpants and planning to swim from the beach back to the Walton Park Hotel, where they were all staying. He struggled against the tide and became stuck in a small bay between the pier and Ladye Bay. His friends raised the alarm and the police helicopter from Portishead arrived, armed with searchlights, followed by an RAF helicopter with a winch. He was hauled to safety and taken to Frenchay Hospital. He survived his ordeal." Linda Strong

"I used to swim from Ladye Bay years ago and had to make sure I kept my mouth closed. I almost bit a Richard the Third once." (In those days sewerage could be dumped in the channel. Nowadays they just go through the motions.)
Doug Gregory

"*Chipping Sodbury Yacht Club is the proud sponsor of a brass plaque on the pier. The club was founded in late 1970s, with the intention of raising funds for charity and generally having a fun time. One condition of membership is that you must not own a boat! The club uniform is white trousers and navy blue blazers and the headquarters is a pub in Chipping Sodbury called the Beaufort Hunt. Important competitions include a round-Ireland yacht race played on a game board and boat races on the River Frome, during which small boats can disappear up a nine-inch pipe. There is also a duck race on a member's pond.*" Linda Strong

"*It was a calm afternoon; the sailing session had finished and we'd just washed the safety boat and stored it away. We were on our way home when we heard someone shouting from the direction of the water. A woman was in trouble, so we rushed back, got the safety boat out again and took it down the slip. The water was low and only just safe enough to launch. We didn't have time to worry about the water level as the woman was being swept downstream on an ebbing tide. Thankfully, we managed to reach her and she was brought ashore without any further mishap.*" Sailing club

"*The rescue boat was launched in response to an emergency phone call from the police, saying that a hot air balloon was flying over from Cardiff. The winds had strengthened and were too strong for the balloon to land in Wales. It flew over the Severn Estuary, somewhere between Black Rock and Portishead, and might not have had sufficient gas to reach the English coast. It was travelling so quickly that the rescue boat couldn't catch it, and occasionally flew so low that the basket dipped into the water. Additional help arrived in the form of the Portishead lifeboat, which managed to get a rope attached to the balloon. When the balloon pilot turned on the burner to stop the balloon from sinking into the river, it took off and lifted the back end of the lifeboat out of the water. The balloon eventually managed to land safely on the Bristol side of the river.*" Sailing club

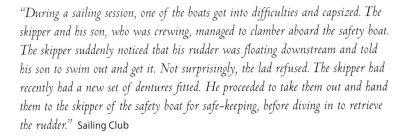

"*During a sailing session, one of the boats got into difficulties and capsized. The skipper and his son, who was crewing, managed to clamber aboard the safety boat. The skipper suddenly noticed that his rudder was floating downstream and told his son to swim out and get it. Not surprisingly, the lad refused. The skipper had recently had a new set of dentures fitted. He proceeded to take them out and hand them to the skipper of the safety boat for safe-keeping, before diving in to retrieve the rudder.*" Sailing Club

"In the same way that the pier creates both a focal point and a challenge for the sailing fraternity, the windsurfers face a similar challenge, particularly with a southwesterly wind. One surfer was blown into the pier, and his board and sail were badly damaged. I received an alarm call and went out in the rescue boat. When I neared the scene I found the surfer clinging to the pier legs. As the incoming tide was flowing at nine knots, I had to be careful that I didn't end up hitting the pier and capsizing. I had a spare lifejacket on board and tied it to a line, which I let drift towards the surfer, shouting at him to grab hold of it. Thankfully the surfer was strong enough to do it and I was able to pull him to safety."
Mark Chislett

THE PIER IN WORDS

One of the first things I notice when stepping onto the pier, are the rows of brass plaques. It is almost impossible to walk by without stopping to read them. At dusk, the scene becomes magical as the low sun illuminates the brass. If the sky contains a mixture of swiftly moving clouds and low sun, it is even more mesmerising – a moving natural spotlight along the promenade.

Fundraising schemes, introduced in the late 1980s, play a vital part in paying for the pier's ongoing upkeep. One such scheme was 'Sponsor a Plank', whereby sponsors paid a sum of money in return for having a brass plaque attached to the pier, inscribed with any wording they wanted – within reason, of course.

Anyone can have a plaque, whether still living or not. Admittedly, it is infinitely more difficult for a person who has passed over to the other side to arrange, but I like to think that where there's a will there's a way! There is seemingly no end to the reasons for having a plaque made. It may be for vanity, a marriage proposal, humour, quirkiness, in celebration, in thanks, or as a memorial. Sometimes it is simply for the fun of it, or perhaps to do a little bit towards the raising of funds. There are those written by or about famous people, loved ones, locals, visitors, pets, organisations, societies, pier-devotees, fishermen and many others.

I could spend days studying the plaques. Each visit fuels a growing desire to discover what lies behind the words. On one occasion, a chance meeting led me to uncover a remarkable story.

At 4pm on November 1st, 2007, I was hurrying to reach the pier in time to catch the last light of the day. I could tell from the sky that there was potential for a great photograph, assuming I found a suitable angle and used the light to my advantage. The tollhouse and shop had just closed, and I was looking for the access code which would allow me to enter by the side gate. I noticed an elderly lady in considerable discomfort as she struggled to walk up the slope to the tollhouse. Although she was supporting herself using a wheeled frame, her progress was much less steady than mine. Her body language suggested total exasperation at the discovery that the pier had closed for the day.

I couldn't help but feel sympathy for her, as it was obvious she had struggled to reach the pier. Her name was Jean and she told me she'd gone against family advice and had walked about a mile and half from her home so that she could reach the pier before it closed. She was recuperating from a serious illness and was learning to walk again.

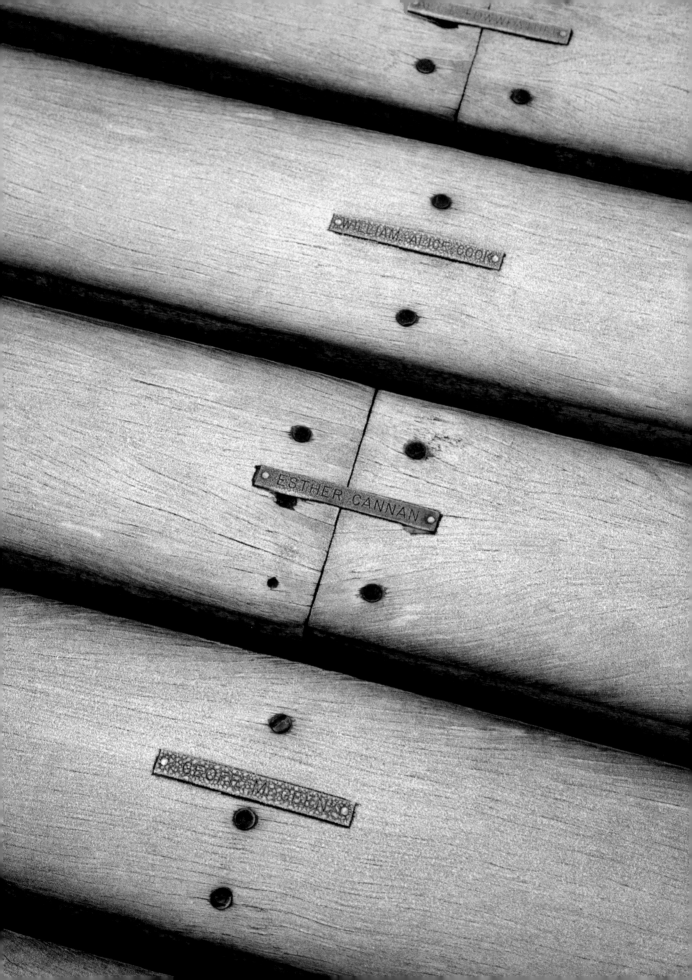

Jean had made an immense effort to visit a brass plaque she had had placed on the pier some nine years earlier. The plaque was a commemoration of the tragic death of Jean's mother, Ellen Elizabeth May Bricknell, in 1938, at the tender age of 39, while carrying her fifth child. Years later, Jean went to visit her mother's grave only to discover that it and many others in the cemetery had been destroyed during the war by a direct hit from a doodlebug. There was no longer a grave to visit.

I met Jean on the anniversary of her mother's death. Each year she visited the plaque to pay her respects to her mother and she would have a photograph taken of herself at either end of the pier to prove that she was there. This was her annual pilgrimage and on this occasion she was to be denied her visit.

As I was listening to what was developing into an extremely moving story, it was becoming obvious that we had a kindred spirit. It was fascinating how many coincidences cropped up in our separate lives. I mentioned that I was

visiting the pier as part of my project to photograph and write a book about the location. Her mood began to change markedly from one of disappointment and frustration to excitement and interest and she began to enthuse about her own previous exploits as a photographer, writer and poet. Jean shed a tear or two and held my hand tightly on several occasions.

While we chatted and I listened to her story, my mind was in turmoil. Jean was standing with her back to the pier and, in a considerate way, apologised for keeping me from my work. I was acutely aware that the sky was rapidly becoming more and more dramatic. I knew that the lights on the pier would be programmed to switch on at any moment and that the 'crossover' light (a combination of natural and artificial light) which all landscape photographers crave was imminent. However, much as I wanted the image I had previsualised, I couldn't bring myself to halt the conversation. I was enjoying listening to her story and felt considerably moved by it.

A moment arose when it seemed right to say goodbye. Hoping I wasn't being too rude, I gave her my business card and she reciprocated with her contact details. My sense of panic rose as I realised I had mislaid the access code for the pier and looked around for someone to help. Then I remembered the 'safe place' and during a frenzied few minutes looked for a suitable composition which would include the incredible light in front of me.

I then had two huge strokes of luck. The plaque which Jean had told me about was easy to locate, but unfortunately its position meant that it was in deep shadow when compared with the relatively bright sky behind. I was aware that the stunning light I had spent nine months pursuing was about to disappear. My first piece of good fortune was that the plaque had been polished only two weeks earlier by one of the pier staff who had kindly offered to help Jean, and stood out from the other tarnished brass plaques nearby. Secondly, I suddenly remembered that I had recently been gifted a torch and had stored it in my camera bag. I was able to illuminate the plaque just sufficiently for it to stand out in the image – it became a focal point.

My overwhelming desire to capture the image for myself had been overtaken by the need to do this for Jean. Almost a week later, I was able to visit her at home and surprise her with a large print of the dramatic scene I had witnessed. Her overjoyed reaction meant much to me. The tragic loss of her mother and unborn baby and the subsequent destruction of her grave meant that Jean had nowhere to visit; there was no final resting place, nowhere to spend quiet, private moments thinking of her mother. The plaque on the pier has provided these opportunities, and means a great deal to Jean. Many other families have benefited in a similar way, and this little piece of Clevedon has become much more than just a pier.

As Jean said: "It is 'OUR PLACE, MUM.'"

 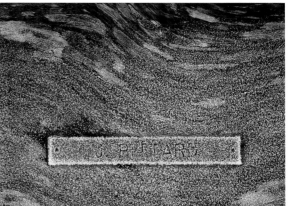

"I met Brian when he was in the army and, two weeks later, on October 16th, 1956, we went out on our first proper date. He had borrowed his auntie's car and collected me, which gave me the impression that he was wealthy. He continued wooing me by giving me a box of Black Magic chocolates. It was a beautiful sunny day and, even now, seems just like yesterday. In the pier head buildings we danced to music - Paul Anka's Dance was our favourite and became our song.

As a surprise for Brian on our golden wedding anniversary, I arranged for a plaque commemorating the event to be installed on the pier. It said, simply: 'Brian & Liz Richards 16/9/56 first date, 17/8/07 golden date'.

The surprise took on even greater meaning when the coach turned up to collect us from home to take us to the pier. On it was a group of friends and relatives who had promised to keep the secret from Brian. I had smuggled in a bottle of champagne in my small shoulder bag and it wasn't until Brian was on board that he became suspicious. When we reached the plaque, friends showered us with confetti and raised a glass in our honour. We were all in tears, even the staff. Linda, the manager, took some photos for the family. It was such a special day for both of us. A framed certificate, replicating the wording of the plaque, hangs on our wall at home." Liz and Brian Richards

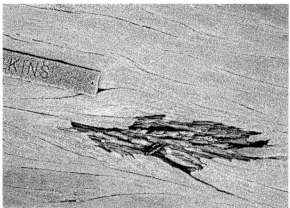

"My father was born in Clevedon and, as a young boy, he would wear holes in the knees of his trousers as, each day, he peeked under the doors of an engine shed to catch a glimpse of the traction engine within. This interest and passion for engines and historical engineering (he was a Brunel enthusiast) became a big part of his life and, in 1972, he purchased a Ruston Proctor agricultural traction engine - the Cornmaiden. He restored it and rallied it across the southwest.

I too lived in Clevedon and, at the time of the pier re-opening, I bought a plaque for my father. Dad liked it - rather like legitimate graffiti! It has now become a memorial headstone to find on every visit to the pier to ponder a while, to reflect and remember.

When I bought the plaque, I sent dad the co-ordinates and a photograph. We had fun finding it on a wonderful trip to the pier, where we sailed on the Waverley with all the family. Seven of us donned boaters, and on a sunny evening, rendezvoused at the pier and climbed aboard for a quick spin around Steep Holm and Flat Holm, returning after a drink or two. The alighting was somewhat precarious and tricky due to the fallen tide - the ascent was dauntingly steep!

These happy memories of our trip from the pier will last forever." Alison Dymond

A CLOSER LOOK

Frost and snow have each left their mark on me. I stood at the shore end of the pier and looked out on a snow-covered promenade. It was immaculate, not one footprint in sight. I couldn't bring myself to walk on it and not just because it would have ruined the image I had in mind. It just felt wrong to spoil such a magical sight.

I had left Bristol in an indecisive mood. Thank goodness I persevered, as I was treated to the only snow covering of the year (of which I am aware). The snow on the shore had already begun to melt, so I knew I didn't have much time in which to compose and make my picture. Thankfully, the pier lights were still on and the first glimmer of light – known as nautical twilight – appeared in the sky. The scene was so beautiful I wished I could have shared the moment with others.

I quickly set up my tripod, composed the picture and had no sooner pressed the shutter than all the pier lights went out. That first frame was my test shot, the idea being that it would give me a better idea of what my final exposure would be. I did take a few more frames, but the magic was gone and I never did get another opportunity. Luckily, the one frame I took was usable and, to my delight, is included in this book.

Each time I step onto the pier it feels as if I'm in another world. I'm on holiday. People smile and talk to one another. I'm away from traffic and, to all intents and purposes, I'm away at sea. Troubles and concerns are left ashore as the movement of tidal water underneath has a calming effect. For some reason it seems much further from the pier head to the shore than the other way round. I've never been able to understand why this is. Perhaps it explains why fishing is so popular and why so many social functions are organised throughout the year. Obviously raising funds for the upkeep of the pier is paramount, but it's the sense of otherworldliness that makes it all so appealing.

What strikes me most about the pier is its simplicity. It has a wonderful Victorian feel to it, with none of the commercial razzamatazz I've seen on others. Two of the longest seats imaginable are interspersed with cast iron lampposts. I was always led to believe that blue and green should never be seen, but I love the way in which the maritime hues of those same colours have been used to great effect. The occasional smallest splash of red jumps out at me, highlighting an ornate piece of ironwork.

My quest for closer, more detailed shots of the pier found me standing on the pier head one bitterly cold winter's morning. Although it was well before

dawn, the frost made the scene appear much lighter than it really was. My mind was miles away, concentrating on making a composition which, ultimately, I abandoned. Something happened which I won't forget in a hurry. I nearly jumped out of my skin when, out of the mist, I saw a hunched figure slowly walking towards me. Half suspecting the tollhouse 'toastie ghostie', of whom not many are aware, I was pleased to find it was no-one more sinister than Rod the fisherman. (I can't help but wonder whether his wife is called Annette…) I'm glad I saw him before he reached me, as I'm sure a gentle tap on my shoulder would have seen me leap over the railings with the next day's newspaper headlines screaming: 'UNHAPPY SNAPPER DISA-PIERS'.

There was always going to be a moment when I had to call a halt to the photography on the pier – when I felt I had sufficient images. Enough was enough! If I hadn't captured the atmosphere and very essence of the pier by this time, then I probably never would. It was 21 December, 2007, and I had been visiting Clevedon on and off for about nine months. After dusk, and to the accompaniment of the Salvation Army band, 200 or so keen but not overly talented carol singers (pardoning a few exceptions, of course) let rip over the ebbing tide, as it were. I arrived intending to take a few photographs using long exposures to recreate the atmospheric scene but, for a change, my camera gear stayed in the bag. I felt moved by the whole event and for the first time in nine months of photographing what used to be 'a rusty heap of old metal', I really did feel enough was enough.

"In the early 1960s, I was a young boy and lived with my family in Norfolk House. My bedroom had a wonderful view, overlooking the pier and passing ships. I used to love looking through my binoculars at the flags on the ships' funnels and work out which country they came from. I was always interested in fishing and spent most of my time on the pier. I learned how to fish from a man called Viv Williams, who had retired from the RAF. He sported an amazing handlebar moustache and spoke in a way you'd imagine a high-ranking person would.

Viv was a great fisherman. He used snooker cues as rods and large wooden reels. He would stay for hours, but never missed his lunchtime ritual at the Pier Hotel. Leaving his rods in position, he would walk back along the pier to the hotel for two hours of drinking, before returning to see if he'd caught anything. In those days we would fish in any conditions, even in force eight gales.

Viv used to hide his fishing gear and bait in the roof of one of the outer shelters, so he didn't have to carry them home. I'm sure only the fisherman knew about the small hatch. His equipment was always there when he returned the next day." John White

"I was in the middle of a particularly busy clinic about ten years ago when the hospital manager, an ex-ward sister of mine who I have known for many years, Gwen Hobbs, interrupted the clinic to ask me what I was intending to do to help fundraise for the new outpatient building! I was somewhat peeved at being interrupted during a busy clinic and uttered the sentence (which I later came to regret): 'What the hell do you think, Gwen? Throw myself off the end of the bloody pier?'

I thought nothing more of it until several months later. One of my regulars visited me in the clinic and, at the end of our consultation, handed me a plastic shopping bag. 'What's in here?' I asked her, and she invited me to take a peek inside. I pulled out a leopard skin leotard and began to wonder whether the consultation was taking a devious turn. 'That's for your pier jump,' she said. 'We all think you're very brave!'

I later found out that Gwen had taken me at my word and, before long, a small publicity machine had started to increase the hype about a jump off the pier by one of their consultants. I had known nothing about it. Needless to say, I couldn't really call their bluff and had to go through with it. I tried on the leotard behind locked doors later that night.

When the day came, I was pleased to note that the tide was fully in. I changed upstairs in the small shop at the end of the pier and walked, rather embarrassed, down the pier, where quite a large crowd had gathered to watch my demise. I was pleased to note a small launch circling in the estuary below, only to be told it was the coastguard rather than the lifeboat. (Lifeboats tend to rescue people; coastguards apparently just pick up bodies!) This did nothing for my confidence. Eventually, after a lot of hype and music, I climbed gingerly up to the top of the handrail and - without spending too long studying the distance between the water and me - hurled myself off. The fall was long enough for me to complete several sentences of expletives before hitting the water. I then remember looking up and seeing the light becoming less... and less... and less... At that point I resolved to lose some weight. Fortunately, before my lungs burst, I began to bob slowly up to the surface, where I heard a round of applause.

The hardest part of the trip was yet to come - and it wasn't the swim to the pebble beach. It was clambering over the beach in a ridiculous leopard skin leotard, collecting funds in a bedpan from a bewildered crowd. However, the end result was very pleasing as we made several thousand pounds for the new outpatient building. I'm not sure what it did for my image, but I'm sure it didn't improve the water quality in the Severn Estuary!" Dr John Harvey

"The fishing competition barbeque - at which there were only two women - was in full flow. Someone shouted to one of the women: 'You'd better take a look at your lines, your rods are bouncing.'

Reeling in their lines excitedly, one found a chicken drumstick on the end, the other a rubber duck!" Linda Strong

"A huge wreath was thrown over the side by an elegant lady. She was seeing her father off well.
Unfortunately, the wreath disintegrated into at least 100 pieces when it hit the water.
'Shit. I paid £50 for that!' she said." Maggie Ashford

"*I went to St Brandon's School at the top of Beach Road, in the grounds of Clevedon Hall. There were about 250 pupils in all, 40 in each year. When the girls left at the end of their final year, it was a tradition to go and throw their felt hats and hymn books into the Bristol Channel from the end of the pier. I distinctly remember the collapse of the pier. I was in London at the time and can recall it being mentioned on the national news.*"

Alison Batchelor

LIFE ON THE BEACH

I remember being disappointed by my first visit to the sea front at Clevedon. The word 'beach' conjured up visions of sand, turquoise water, blue skies, ice cream and the occasional rush of blood to the head while diving headlong into the waves. It wasn't like that at all – but it did have a special charm of its own. You could – and still can – buy an ice cream under a blue sky! There was no sand, but there were millions of pebbles, rocks, odd bits of driftwood and plenty of seaweed. Oh, and a pier. What more could a photographer wish for?

People – romantic couples – promenaded along the sea front or down the slipway to watch a setting sun. Camera flashguns lit up all of ten feet of foreground, much to my amusement. Barbeques, picnics, ball games, pebbles being thrown into the sea or skimmed across the top of as many waves as possible were just a few of the ways that people were enjoying their time on the beach. Some were happy to sit and watch the world go by. Others engaged in more bizarre activities – I was once serenaded by a duet of duelling didgeridoos, although I'm not sure that 'serenaded' is the right word.

My passion for photography has changed my view of the beach, and now I look forward to each visit. Taking a stroll down the slipway or watching the action from the esplanade has been a great experience. The slipway has been a revelation for me. I didn't realise there was such an abundance of crabs scuttling among the seaweed as the tide comes in. On a summer's day, parents and children compete to see who can catch the most and the largest. Avoiding getting a soaking was all part of the fun. I had lots of laughs watching others play King Canute with the waves. Those who didn't react quickly enough to escape the oncoming water always took it with good humour – not that they had any choice.

Photographing people on the beach and esplanade was entirely candid. I wanted to show the subjects enjoying themselves. Beaches are fun places and this was evident in the majority of those I saw. If I had adopted a different approach, asked permission and then taken photographs from a much closer viewpoint, their behaviour would have been different. Very few people are able to act naturally once they are aware that a camera is being pointed in their direction.

Occasionally, I met other photographers on the esplanade overlooking the beach, usually at dusk, and enjoyed a chinwag with them. Passers-by, too, are often intrigued at the sight of a large tripod supporting a lengthy lens. They wondered what I was photographing and some would say, "Nice day for

photography." It was always friendly and I didn't have the heart to reply, "Actually, it isn't," but I knew what they meant. I took it as a compliment when someone asked if they could look through my lens.

That wasn't the case when I watched one photographer set up his camera. It was a large format (10x8in) camera, which needed a robust tripod to support it. I would have been proud to own such a beautifully-crafted piece of equipment, and it reminded me of the excellent work of the American photographer, Ansel Adams. The camera was so large that, when the bellows were fully extended, the photographer had to take several steps forward to reach the front of the lens. As he went under the black cloth (which kept out light) to fine-tune his focusing, an excitable onlooker invited himself under the cloth, saying, "What's going on here then?" He was swiftly encouraged to go about his business elsewhere.

If I lived locally, I would be out early each morning to see what the tide had brought in, or what holidaymakers had left. I have been fascinated to learn about some of the finds – furniture, clothing, pallets, money and trees. Unfortunately, I've not found anything more interesting than a couple of empty crisp packets.

"I'm 67 now and have always been accident-prone. When I was 17, my friends and I used to go dancing at the disco on the pier head - also to a nearby club at the Salthouse - and generally enjoy flirting with the boys on the sea front, near the pier. Not only were there the young men of Clevedon to choose from, but a group of potential young suitors used to travel by bus from Portishead, further up the Bristol Channel. We didn't drink alcohol but were happy enough dancing to rock 'n' roll and drinking Coca-Cola. Mr Faraday, who looked after the pier in those days, even trusted us with the keys.

One day, I was dressed in a brand new pink, pencil thin dress and high heels (all of which were a treat from my mother). I was accompanied by a crowd of my girlfriends, who were showing off to a group of boys on the sea front. I began to run down the slipway towards the sea dodging the waves - the inevitable happened and I slipped and fell, and ended up getting a good soaking, much to the hilarity of the others. One of my friends had to escort me back home and help me face my mother - not a lady to be reckoned with. I ended up in deep trouble, not to mention with hurt pride! The dress was ruined." **Ann Melluish**

"From the shop window, I saw a couple sitting on the slipway. They first walked their pram and well-wrapped bundle down the beach into the sea, before going up to the pier and asking if it was OK to walk along it. I told them it was - and noticed that the bundle contained a cat! This happened for three years, but on the last year the bundle had become a baby. They came from Bristol." Maggie Ashford

"I once found a left shoe on the beach - it had a foot in it. Then I found another shoe in the same area, but it was also for the left foot." Maggie Ashford

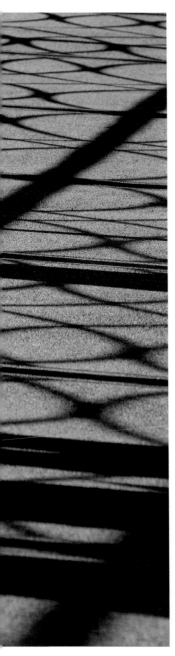

"The area down by the beach is well-known locally for not having a strong radio and TV signal. Some houses can only receive Welsh television channels from across the channel. The late Roger Bennett, the BBC Radio Bristol presenter, struggled to broadcast his popular breakfast show from the esplanade behind the beach. Technology came to his aid as the signal was bounced across to Wales and back to the Bristol area. It was the day before the pagoda re-opened following its restoration." 'Taxi' Tim Vine

"I remember when the Waverley captain gave permission for the first officer to bring the boat up to the pier. She was doing very well, but unfortunately forgot there were large paddle wheels on the side of the boat. She smashed the boat into the concrete pier head and has never been seen since. In her defence, there may have been very little current at the time, which would have helped her use the rudder."
John, the 'sea hobbler'

"Almost every time I have visited Clevedon beach, I've seen people having fun throwing pebbles into the sea, reminding me of happy times spent on family holidays when I was young. I would pick up pebbles and see how many times I could get them to bounce on the water's surface. Skimming was something I was quite good at and, being competitive, I always had to try and out-do my father. We would try and count the number of bounces, but sometimes this was impossible." Clive Minnitt

NATURAL ELEMENTS

Words by Charles Copp. Few among the many thousands of visitors to Clevedon are aware of the amazing story that is written in the local rocks and landscape. This is a story that ranges back over 400 million years and includes changes in the environment from hot deserts, to tropical seas, steamy swamps and frozen glacial wastes.

The earth is never still and movements below the crust split the continents, moving them around until they crush together, creating mountains. In the past 400 million years 'Clevedon' has moved from south of the equator, crossing different climatic belts while the earth itself has gone through hot periods and, more recently, very cold periods. On the way its rocks have been added to, folded and faulted, uplifted and eroded – and we are still moving.

Changes in the level of the land, and the amount of ice at the poles, result in huge relative changes of sea level. As recently as 18,000 years ago, local sea level was some 130m lower than it is now. Even 7,000 years ago pine trees grew way out into what is now the Severn Estuary. However, when we look at erosion levels on local hills and around the Mendips, we find evidence that sea levels have even been more than 100m higher than at present. The road level along Clevedon sea front and the low cliff platform north of Ladye Bay marks the remains of a beach, some five metres above current sea level, dating back to the last Interglacial period 125,000 years ago – so changing sea levels are nothing new!

On Clevedon beach you can see the evidence for this amazing history. One of the clearest features is the small promontory on which the Victorian pier was built. The wall of rock under the pier has been pushed up by a fault whose line can be traced all the way along Alexandra Road, opposite. This fault line was important because it allowed mineral-rich fluids to rise up from deep down and to percolate through the overlying rocks. The main mineralisation includes ores of barium, lead, copper and zinc – the most easily spotted being the pink-coloured barytes (barium sulphate) and silver-grey galena (lead sulphide). This suite of minerals also reacted with seawater to produce a range of rare secondary minerals, one of the reasons why the 'Pier Vein' is protected as a national Site of Special Scientific Interest (SSSI).

Another interesting feature of the rocks under the pier is what is called an angular unconformity. The rocks in the lowermost corner of the beach are red-brown sandstones of Lower Devonian age, deposited in a huge, semi-arid river basin around 400 million years ago. Overlying the Devonian at this point we

Above: shallow marine sediments that show fossil ripple marks (in the lighter coloured sediment) deposited in beach and near shore conditions at the beginning of the Carboniferous period.

have yellowish, sandy limestones and boulder deposits laid down perhaps 220 million years ago in the Triassic period, a time when the Severn Estuary would have more resembled Death Valley, California. The boulder deposits are called the dolomitic conglomerate, and represent debris fans that bordered the hills of the arid Severn Valley at a time when dinosaurs were just evolving.

This means that the line between the Triassic rocks and the underlying Devonian marks the erosion of everything that was deposited in the intervening 150 million-plus years! You can get an idea of what some of the missing rocks were like by walking south, along the beach towards the sailing club. As you pass the slipway you can see near vertical beds of rock running out to sea. These beds at first appear sandy but as you approach the sailing club they appear more limey and fossils start to appear, mainly the small, round stem ossicles of crinoids, also called sea lilies. The low cliff just beyond the sailing club is full of fossils, including small corals and shells called brachiopods. These changes mark rising sea levels and the deposition of beach and shallow sea sediments at the time that marks the change from the Upper Devonian to the Carboniferous period, around 360 million years ago.

Seen from the air, Clevedon beach is not just a simple succession of beds from one end to the other; instead, the beds appear to swing around in zigzag arcs which are sometimes cut through by lines that displace beds relative to one another. This is because the beds have been folded, faulted and tilted so that subsequent erosion (creating the beach) slices across them. In fact, careful study shows that the sequence of beds is repeated more than once by the faulting. One of the best places to see the folding clearly is in Little Harp Bay, by the bandstand. All this folding and faulting is related to a period of mountain building called the Variscan or Hercynian Orogeny, which took place in phases throughout the Devonian and Carboniferous periods, culminating around 300 million years ago with movements that created the Mendips and the hills surrounding Clevedon. It was on these hills that dinosaurs and the earliest known mammals walked some 200 million years ago.

The evidence for what happened over the next 200 million years can be found in rocks all round the Bristol district, but have long since been removed by erosion around Clevedon. One incredible result of the burial of the old Triassic valleys and hills with sediments deposited by rising sea levels in the following Jurassic period is that when these sediments were eventually eroded away (by uplift associated with the formation of the Alpine mountains) the ancient landscape was once more exposed. When you look around at the landscape of Clevedon, you are essentially looking at the fossilised landscape of 200 million years ago – now clothed in trees, grass and houses.

Above: lower Devonian sandstone (c400 million years old) deposited by a large seasonal river flowing over a flood plain towards a huge delta situated where north Devon is now.

Opposite: the lowermost Carboniferous beds include many crystal-lined holes, which may be due to minerals (calcite) filling cavities left by the solution of evaporite minerals (such as gypsum) from shoreline sediments in a hot climate. This is part of the evidence for the transition from continental deposits of the Devonian into marine deposits of the Lower Carboniferous caused by a world rise in sea levels 360 million years ago.

Above: another view of the lowermost Carboniferous beds.

Opposite: another fault runs behind the sailing club (you can trace it also in the road opposite) and uplifts the low cliff of Carboniferous limestone. These rocks are more fully marine and full of fossils of corals, crinoids and brachiopods.

Opposite: sedimentary process can be seen fossilised in the rocks (boulders and cobbles in the Triassic dolomitic conglomerate and also in the underlying Devonian) and still in action on the modern beach. This picture shows what we call a wave-cut platform (which can also be seen in local fossilised raised beaches as between Ladye Bay and Portishead). It also shows rounded cobbles (actually it is interesting to see how the waves sort the pebbles by size on the beach) and muddy sand here shaped into what we call bow-shaped linguoid ripples. (Tells you something about the direction and velocity of the water.)

"When we arrived at the pier each morning, it seemed to be an automatic reaction to study the beach or to marvel at the height of the tide. One could tell so much about the events of the previous evening by just scanning the pebbles. The loveliest sight must be the fairly small expanse of beach that had been cleansed by a retreating high tide, as yet untouched by man or dog. Each pebble would shine right at you as though it was saying thank you. There was also the opposite vista, when an angry tide was followed by a high wind - sometimes at gale force - bringing with it all manner of rubbish, most of it plastic." Maggie Ashford

AND FINALLY…

Political, economic and environmental pros and cons aside, if the proposal to build a barrage across the Severn Estuary in order to provide electricity for the region ever comes to fruition, it will alter the nature of the tidal flows in the Bristol Channel. The area of land which lies between low and high water marks, known as the inter-tidal range, will undoubtedly change – who knows whether for better or worse?

The role of this book has changed since its conception. It has become more than a collection of photographs and anecdotes, and is now an important means of recording the way the channel, the pier and the bay appeared in 2007. It now has historical value. I have often felt – as I stood on the seafront and marvelled at the pier's construction, its wonderfully skilled restoration and its glorious setting – that nothing is forever.

I hope the readers of this book make a point of visiting the seafront at Clevedon and spend time looking out towards the pier. Think about what it stands for – and imagine what it would be like without it.

Hats off to all those who planned it, designed it, built it, ran it, argued for it, funded it, re-built it, used it, worked on it, wrote about it, painted it, photographed it, or just stood and gazed at it – it really is worth preserving.

"One woman who came to visit the pier, said as she left: 'I don't think much of it here – there's not even a whelk stall.'" 'Taxi' Tim Vine

"It's often said in Clevedon that most of the town's adults will have been conceived on the pier." Rosemary Rumour

PHOTOGRAPHER'S NOTES

All the photographs in this book were made between March 2007 and January 2008.

Camera: Canon EOS 5D, 12.8 megapixel body.
Lenses: 16-35mm L USM, 24-105mm L USM IS, 100-400mm L USM IS, 1.4x Converter. All Canon lenses.
Filters: 0.3, 0.6 and 0.9 neutral density filters; 0.3, 0.6 and 0.9 neutral density graduated filters – both hard and soft – all by Lee Filters. 105mm circular polariser by Heliopan.
Tripod: Manfrotto 055 PROB with Manfrotto 410 head. Apart from the people shots, all images were taken using a tripod, so that camera shake was reduced to a minimum. I also benefited from being able to spend more time considering the composition and light while the camera was being supported.

Lighting: Almost all images were photographed in either natural daylight or using the pier lights – or a combination of both. The one exception was the image on page 54 where a pocket torch was used to illuminate the single plaque.
Camera Bag: Lowepro AW Trekker II.
Image workflow: RAW and JPEG files were simultaneously produced in camera. The RAW files were loaded into Canon converter software before basic work was completed on each image in Adobe Photoshop CS3. This included dust spot removal, brightness, contrast, highlight and shadow details, and finally sharpening. The files were saved as printable TIFF files.

THE IMAGES

P1. Soft early evening light created a mood of relaxation. It was a stroke of luck that the two figures moved into exactly the right position, creating a continuation of the lamp pattern. Thankfully, I had anticipated their moves correctly and wasted no time in pressing the shutter.

P3. The dramatic sky emphasised the pagoda's dominance. The sepia toning was carried out in camera.

P3. Two excellent relationships immediately caught my eye – the complementary colours of red and green, and the two red crosses. I used a fast shutter speed so the flag and sea would appear as life-like as possible.

P9. I had to work quickly to capture the images I had in mind. The frost would soon melt, the lights would be timed to switch off and the first footprints would spoil the sense of solitude. Using an extreme wide angle lens allowed me to create the impression of space between the plaques and the distant pagoda. I chose these particular plaques because of the interesting marks on the planks nearby.

P10. My favourite subjects to photograph are landscapes and architecture. At one stage I became aware that I hadn't included many people in the images. The pier is such a popular venue that I didn't want to portray it as soulless. The arrival of the Balmoral gave me the opportunity I needed.

P12. The Barlow rails used to construct the pier legs were a great source of photographic material. People clambered onto them to shout support to swimmers taking part in the Clevedon Long Swim and became excellent subjects in their own right. I had to react quickly to capture the relationship between the swimmer's arms and the pier leg supports.

P13. A dull day is not always a non-productive day. The red sails livened up the scene and the registration codes added interest. The old adage, 'less is more', worked. Including small sections of the three nearest boats leads the eye to the dinghy in action.

P15. Looking like someone has spent far too much time on the pier, the wet weather gear belonged to a fisherman who was packing up to go home. This was a handheld shot taken in a hurry.

P17. As Clevedon is known for its sunsets, I felt it was important that I included a version of my own. Watching the local weather forecast meant I was able to plan my visit to coincide with the arrival of the Balmoral steamer. Once the sun had dropped below the horizon I was rewarded with a dramatic sky.

P18. Some of my favourite images were made when the tide was incoming and the surf was pounding the rocks underneath the pier. It was exhilarating working under such conditions. There was too much contrast between shadow and highlight areas in this scene and I had to place five stops of graduated neutral density filter over the sky to record detail in all areas.

P21. Long exposures and swiftly moving clouds work together well, especially at dusk when the sky is full of warm colours.

P22. Soft early evening light was sufficiently strong to produce a shadow of the pier on the water. This is one of the most frequently photographed views of the pier.

P23. This scene consisted of mainly bright subject matter. Therefore, I had to override the camera's metering system and overexpose by one stop to avoid the image looking grey.

P24-25. Photographing the same subject from a similar vantage point on different days shows the vast changes in conditions.

P27. The few elements that make up this scene have been carefully placed for maximum impact. If the silhouetted land mass had been a less pleasing shape I would not have included it.

P29. Low tide in the Bristol Channel often conjures up an image of ugly mud flats. Using shape, textures and gorgeous, evocative light, it is possible to show how beautiful the area is.

P31. It was a rainy day, but photography was still possible. This was taken from inside my (parked) car, focusing on the windscreen in the near foreground. The blue boat adds a splash of colour to the scene.

P32. Constant spray was causing problems, making it imperative that I dried my lens between each frame. Shielding the tripod and camera from the strong wind eradicated camera shake and enabled me to use a long shutter speed to show the movement of water on the rocks.

P33. Cameras and sea water do not mix well – it was a case of trial and error until one particular wave crashed on the sea wall and created the effect I was looking for. By increasing the ISO and using a fast shutter speed I was able to 'freeze' the water at its highest point. I felt for those who got a soaking.

P34. When setting up this image, it took me a long time to achieve a composition with which I was pleased. I arrived an hour before I eventually pressed the shutter and during that time the light got better and better. The foreground light source was from within the pagoda.

P35. A long lens (100-400mm) enabled me to study the wave patterns at close quarters. Low tide meant that the pier wasn't buffeted by waves, which would have caused it to shudder and the camera to shake.

P37. The decision I had to make was where to place the Balmoral. Many would have put the boat in the centre of the picture. The ratio of sea to land and sky was also considered.

P39. Backlit subjects are very appealing. I had to ensure there was no flare in the lens as a result of photographing directly into the sun and I wanted a gap between the two dinghies. I was intrigued by the way each dinghy was lit and the shadows they formed.

P41. There was a sense of purpose in the way the swimmers approached the water and yet I detected an air of apprehension. I had to react quickly to their movements while trying to create a meaningful composition.

P42. Harsh, full-on light is my least favourite as it results in deep shadows and squinted eyes.

P43. Separating the individuals in the group was difficult without resorting to making a formal announcement and losing any sense of spontaneity that one associates with candid photography.

P43. We all want to take pictures! I included a small section of pier and used a wide aperture to render it out of focus. This gave the pirate figure more dominance.

P45. When photographed on its own, a single canoeist occupying a large expanse of open water doesn't sound like a good idea. However, used in conjunction with another powerful element and atmospheric lighting, its separation became its strength.

P46. 'The camera never lies' was a phrase used regularly before digital photography. Although complicated image manipulation was always possible in the darkroom, state of the art computer software has made it even more so. Not so here – the balloons marked the end of the Clevedon Long Swim.

P47. We all need a bit of luck. A split second before I pressed the shutter the topmost swimmer turned and faced away from the others but remained in a straight line and a uniform distance from the others.

P48. Timing is crucial to the success of an image. Concentrating on the movement of each dinghy, as well as trying to keep an eye on the shape of the whole group, would have been complicated enough. There was also the position of the red sail relative to the rest, plus the relationship of the group to the pier. I think I have achieved partial success, having a gap between each dinghy. A gripe is that I didn't wait for a gap between the right-hand dinghy and the pier.

P49. Burnt out highlights are best avoided. When there is a bright spot in the centre of an image it isn't possible to use a graduated neutral density filter to reduce the brightness without affecting other areas. The inclusion of the dinghy in front of the brightest area rescued the image from mediocrity.

P51. The plaques were fun to photograph. A covering of frost was a bonus and gave a softer overall look. Tight composition was important with extra care taken around the edges of the frame.

P52. Restricting the image to a small part of the plaque forces the viewer to use their imagination. The posy of fresh flowers placed on the seat below was quite moving.

P53. It was easy to miss the plaques set on the base of the lamps. I used a wide lens aperture to throw the background out of focus and this added a bit of mystery. The blue plaque provided a wonderful contrast to the dull colours of the bed of the channel.

P54. 'Our place, Mum'. See 'The Pier in Words'.

P57. Illuminated by the lamps on the pier head, a long exposure was necessary to capture this scene.

P58-59. A single plaque is not particularly photogenic. I searched for those that had been set in wood close to interesting knots, grain or colour.

P61. To make an image more dynamic, one option is to use a wideangle lens and photograph from a point close to the subject. In this image, the plaque is the focal point but I have used the lines of the seats and planks to draw attention to the distant pagoda.

P63. Although this is an uncluttered image I still had to consider many things when making my composition. The sky, the distant land, railings, planks, lamp and fishing rod all had to work together. The rod was photographed as I found it.

P65. I mentioned in the chapter, 'A Closer Look', that no sooner had I taken this single frame, than all the lights went out. I didn't know it at the time but it turned out to be the only occasion that snow fell during the production of this book. A small mount of flare on the lens had to be tidied up in Photoshop.

P67. If the sky doesn't add anything then why include it? It was a miserable day but perfect for reflections on the promenade. A long exposure ensured movement was captured in the flag and visitors.

P68. Dusk and good evening light gave me an opportunity to photograph the pier without having its physical structure in the picture. The conditions were excellent – calm water and a high tide.

P69. Rough seas, delicate pier and low contrast light – simple ingredients but a challenge to transform them into an image. I spent about an hour fine-tuning this composition until I was happy with it. A minute change in camera angle would have thrown the balance out completely.

P70. An unusual angle, this photograph was taken from the gardens opposite the pier. A 100-400mm lens was used to foreshorten the scene and create an image made up almost entirely of vertical lines.

P70. This ornate iron work on the pier head was photographed using light from the pier lamps.

P72. Perfect symmetry was difficult to achieve but was important for the image to work. Using a wideangle lens allowed me to show the gaps between the planks which were directly above where I was standing, as well as the distant pier head.

P73. A calm, featureless sea has given the impression that the pier is hanging in mid air. I included a small amount of reflection to show the reality.

P74. The island of Steep Holm in the distance draws the eye, led by the diagonal rail. The crossover light was beautiful, with different light sources combining to wonderful effect.

P75. A richly-coloured sky at dusk, seen through the pagoda windows, provided an excellent subject. The precise positioning of the foreground window frame was important.

P77. Constantly moving elements – father, children and the sea – and the relationship between the three people and the pier were all considered before pressing the shutter. I like the way the shape of the family unit echoes that of the pier.

P79. Capturing a moment in time – this took me several attempts. The stance of the dog owner, the dog's leap and the position of the ball all worked together once only.

P79. I was fascinated by how the two swimmers (contemplating their next move) and the dog (ready to pounce on the stick) were oblivious to each other and yet so close. A grab shot using a fast shutter speed with image stabilizing switched on.

P80. The pigeons that frequent the holes in the sea wall attracted my attention. I used a long lens and a wide aperture to reduce the depth of field, and waited patiently for the right moment.

P81. A hint of ironwork stimulates one's imagination to wonder what the rest of the pier looks like.

P82. Strong shadows – a result of the light from the setting sun falling on the esplanade railings – provided numerous opportunities to work with shapes and patterns. The relaxed stance of the figure added a holiday mood.

P83. The first thing that caught my eye was the way in which the legs formed a continuation of the rocks. The image makes me want to ask questions about the people, the games and the beach.

P84. Although their facial expressions are not visible, the actions of the children throwing pebbles into the sea speak of fun and competitive enjoyment.

P85. People love to watch the sea from the relative safety of the slipway. Seeing father and daughter enjoying a quiet time together was quite moving and I felt I was intruding on a private moment. The father's protective, caring hand, drawing his daughter towards him, makes the picture.

P87. I was intrigued by the way the falling tide left various elements in its wake. The seaweed appeared to have been carefully draped around a large rock, while the smaller pebbles seem abandoned.

P88. The tidal currents left behind these shapely ridges which, when illuminated by low sunlight, became a series of highlights and shadows. I used a shallow depth of field to bring attention to the single pebble.

P89. There was a huge variety of shapes, textures and colours in a relatively small area (some 6ft sq). An overcast sky results in more saturated colours.

P90. The KISS technique (Keep It Simple, Stupid) has been used with these images. Deciding what to leave out of each composition was more difficult than choosing what to put in.

P92. This image illustrates opposites – weak and strong, large and small, rough and smooth – using the geological features of the beach.

P93. Everyone has their own idea of what makes a good composition. There is no right and wrong as it is so subjective. I spent quite a while deciding how to compose this image so that the loose, flat rock played a meaningful role. I wonder if I have succeeded?

P94. If the dinghies had not been present I would not have included any sea or sky. If you cover both of these, it is interesting how different the image looks.

P95. A stormy sea created a criss-cross pattern with the upturned rock ledges, adding an extra dimension to the picture.

P96. This pool is the largest on the beach and its size is exaggerated through the use of a wideangle lens, making the pier seem further away than it is in reality. Blue sky and white clouds reflected beautifully.

P97. The gentle curve of protruding sand mounds help lead the eye to the reflection of the railings. Crucially, the mounds were pointing in the same direction as the ironwork.

P99. It was a cold, bleak day – exactly what I wanted the image to portray. But, I wonder, why didn't the snow settle in the hollows?

P101. The colours reflecting off the pier were spellbinding. It was before dawn, and my concentration was broken only by the occasional "good morning" from a passing runner, dog walker or cyclist.

P103. Standing on the pier looking north, clouds appeared from the west and gave me the detail I needed in the sky.

P104. I have mentioned the importance of the quality of light many times in this book. The light in this image is wonderful. Although this is a busy image, I can sense a calmness in the bird and the overall feeling is one of serenity.

P107. My eye was caught by the relationship between the angle of the snagged tree and the ironwork of the pier head.

P109. This is one of my favourite images. I love simple, strong lines and relating diagonals. The presence of the broom made a huge difference to the image. After taking this picture I removed it and took another. It lacked something – maybe I had already made up my mind to give it the brush off.

PIER PLAQUES

The character of the pier is reflected in this small selection of plaques.

HAPPY MEMORIES OF MUM & DAD
CHOONG FOONG KOW AND LOKE YANG SENG
WITH LOVE FROM ALL THE FAMILY

JOHN BUTTER
10TH AUGUST 1926 – 2ND JUNE 2004
A GOOD PLACE TO CAPSIZE

MANY HAPPY HOURS SPENT HELPING TO
RESTORE CLEVEDON PIER
ANDY BRIAN
'A HANDSOME LAD'

MIKE REID, JULY 2003

PEANUT

JOHN CRAVEN, BBC TV, COUNTRYFILE
DECEMBER 2005

PUGSLEY CAT
HE SNOOZES ON

ELIZABETH OWEN
MY MOST BEAUTIFUL SUNSET
LOVE ALWAYS, ROB

GRANDMA SUZI, MADE US LAUGH
AND WE STILL DO
XXXXXX

ROY 'PADDY' SILK
LONDONER WHO LOVED THIS PIER
1909 – 2004

CRAZY_RAY
YOU ARE THE SPROUTS TO MY GRAVY
SADFERRET XXX

NEIL & JULIE
OUR PLACE FOR THINKING AND DREAMING

FRANK THE PLANK

GRIFF RHYS JONES

LINDA'S PLAICE

LEN HURLEY – COMMEMORATING
50 CONSECUTIVE CLEVEDON LONG SWIMS
1957 – 2007
CONGRATULATIONS FROM MIDDLE YEO

DONNA PERAY
I WON'T ASK YOU AGAIN
MARRY ME (?)

KEITH WORKMAN
NOTHING BEATS A GOOD DAY'S FISHING

PAULINE MARGARET DANDO 58 YEARS
A LOVELY LADY WITH A BIG SMILE WHO HAD
A PASSION FOR MUSIC, CHOCOLATE AND
HER DUVET

CLIVE RAYMENT – SAW THE PIER COLLAPSE
AND WAS LATE FOR SCHOOL

Further reading

Clevedon Pier, by Keith Mallory
Redcliffe Press, 1981
ISBN 0 9482 6515 9

Striding Boldly: The Story of Clevedon Pier, by
Nigel Combes
Clevedon Pier Trust Ltd, 1995
ISBN 0 9525 2160 1

The Dinner Lady and Other Women
Bristol Broadsides, 1986 (includes Jean Wythe's
story, Bright Star)
ISBN 0 9069 4426 0

The following books have proved inspirational,
showing that it is possible to produce a body
of work based on a limited subject area:
Roseberry Topping, by Ian Pearce (editor) and
Joe Cornish (photographer)
Great Ayton Community Archeological Project,
2006
ISBN 0 9554 1530 6

The End of the Land, by Andrew Nadolski
Headon House, 2005
ISBN 0 9519 2440 1

I have learnt much from the following two
books:
The Making of Landscape Photographs, by
Charlie Waite
Collins & Brown, 1993
ISBN 1 8558 5149 0

Seeing Landscapes, by Charlie Waite
Collins & Brown, 2002
ISBN 1 8558 5711 1

www.clevedonpier.com
www.minnitt.co.uk

Acknowledgements

While every effort has been made to ensure the
accuracy of the text and stories written by him
and acquired from others, the author apologies
for any errors which may have caused offence
in any way.

I would like to pay tribute to the many
determined people, past and present, who
have contributed to Clevedon Pier, in particular
the Elton Family of Clevedon Court. Without
them neither the pier nor this book would exist.

I have been touched by the help and support
from so many people, notably Clevedon Pier
Board of Trustees for their permission to access
and photograph the pier at all times; Linda
Strong, the current pier manager, for believing
in me and for her unstinting support; Mary
Buck, Ryan Collier, and the many volunteers
who keep the pier and heritage centre going.

I am extremely grateful to Griff Rhys Jones for
writing the foreword. His style of comedy has
long appealed to my sense of humour and his
expert presentation of the BBC's Restoration
series made him the perfect choice to join me
in presenting this book.

I must say a big thank you to landscape
photographer, Charlie Waite, for being such an
inspiration and a good friend. I will always be
grateful to him and Sue Bishop for setting up
Light and Land, the UK's foremost photographic
holiday company. Together with my great chum
and fellow leader, Phil Malpas, I have been let
loose on many unsuspecting clients.

I am greatly indebted to Phil for his
camaraderie, ability to pass on his immense
knowledge of all things photographic and for
accurately recounting amusing tales of my
many faux pas.

I bow down to Phil, Joe Cornish, David Ward,
Eddie Ephraums and Richard Childs – fellow
members of the world famous yet unassuming
CUBS Photographic Society – for their ability to

make me laugh, enjoy an adventure or two and for teaching me new expletives when one of us gets THE picture!

Huge thanks go to Eddie Ephraums for his expert design skills and guiding hand with this book. It has been tremendous fun.

Grateful thanks to Ailsa McWhinnie for her excellent proof-reading.

Also, many thanks to:
Kerry Banner at Daymen International, for supplying my ultra-reliable Lowepro camera bag and Manfrotto tripod.

Andy Brindle, and all at Clifton Colour in Bristol for outstanding service.

Calumet, Bristol, for supplying my trusty Canon cameras and lenses, and always being helpful.

Rob Cook, Paramo Outdoor Clothing, for providing excellent outdoor clothing. Charles Copp, for his wealth of geological knowledge of the area and his contribution to the chapter 'Natural Elements'.

The many enthusiastic 'volunteers' from Clevedon and further afield, who all succumbed to my constant badgering for anecdotes: Maggie Ashford (retired pier mistress), 'Taxi' Tim Vine, John White, Mark Chislett, Alison Dymond, Ray Thomas, Alf Watts, Ann Melluish, Angela Kell, Alexandra Webber, Jerry Turner, Liz and Brian Richards, Doug Gregory, John the Sea Hobbler, Maggie Walker, John Harvey, Jenny Pritchard, Mike Lord, Peter Ruck, the Sailing Club, swimmers and fishermen – all of whom have as much affection for the pier as I have. Sincere apologies to those I may have inadvertently missed and to those who contributed but whose words have not been included purely for reasons of lack of space.

Those of you who have unknowingly had their photograph taken and included in this book – I hope you accept my apologies for intruding on your personal space.

I am also greatly indebted to:
Jean Wythe, for her spirit, determination and moving story.

Gerald and Maggie Hudson, for their great friendship, encouragement and invaluable help.

Steve Hudson, for designing my website www.minnitt.co.uk.

John Ellin, for rescuing me from despair whenever my computer needed a bit of TLC.

Natalie Donbavand, Indira and Bob Suter, and Jayne Burton, who all helped address my lack of wordiness, like wot I must improve.

David and Frances Parr for endless support, and to David for thinking up the book's title.

Sally Packer, who has constantly supplied me with ideas.

John and June Mason, who have expertly printed and supplied business literature.

The many close friends, family members and neighbours who have constantly given me their encouragement, support, food and a bed for the night. You are very much appreciated.

My good lady, Anne, for always being there and being so understanding and enthusiastic about my passion for photography.

My wonderful parents, Denis and Pam, who have always encouraged me to pursue my dreams and helped in endless ways.

My dear sister, Jane, and her daughter, Laura, who tragically lost their lives so young – this book is for you both.

First published in 2008 by Clive Minnitt,
15 Longfield Road, Bishopston, Bristol. BS7 9AG.
Copyright © 2008 by Clive Minnitt
www.minnitt.co.uk

A catalogue record of this book is available from the British Library.

ISBN-13 978-0-9541011-3-8

Printed by DeckersSnoeck. Belgium.

Designed by Eddie Ephraums.
www.envisagebooks.com